Helping Hands

Eric Christopher Meyer

Rigby

A Harcourt Achieve Imprint

www.Rigby.com
1-800-531-5015

Whenever you need help, there's something you should do.

Ask someone to lend a hand. Helping hands are here for you!

When you have a job, a job that's hard to do . . .

Ask someone to help.
Four hands are better than two!

When you want to learn a thing that's very new . . .

Ask someone to help.
Four hands are better than two!

When you have a project, or something fun to do . . .

Ask someone to help.
Four hands are better than two!

And if you're hurt or sick, or feeling a little blue . . .

Ask someone to help.
Four hands are better than two!

And if you see a friend with a job that you can do . . .

Now **you** can help.
Four hands are better than two!

There's one last thing to know, when there's work to do.

When you lend a hand to others . . .

They'll lend a hand to you!